SCIENCE
in the GARDEN

by REBECCA B. MARCUS

Pictures by JO POLSENO

FRANKLIN WATTS, INC.
575 Lexington Avenue • New York 22

FIRST PRINTING
Library of Congress Catalog Card Number: 61-9865
Copyright © 1961 by Franklin Watts, Inc.
Printed in the United States of America
by The Moffa Press, Inc.

The garden is so pretty in the sunshine! Green leaves and lovely flowers make you want to go in and look around.

Maybe you are looking at a garden that has vegetables growing in it as well as flowers. Or there might be an apple tree with ripe apples growing on it. You might also see a bee buzzing around a flower. And a robin might be hunting worms on the grass.

As you look at the garden, have you ever wondered —

What makes the plants grow? Why do they all have leaves?

Why do many plants die in the autumn? Are trees without leaves in the winter really dead?

Are bees and birds of any use to the plants?

Let's find out some things about a garden.

First, just walk around the garden and look at the different kinds of plants. Some are tall, and some short. Some have flowers, some just have pretty leaves. But no matter how different they look, all green plants have —

Leaves

Stems, and

Roots

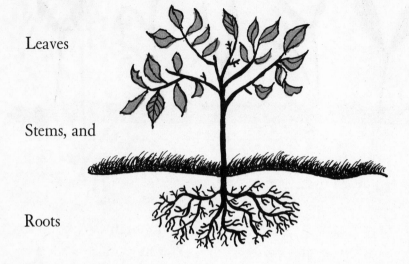

Let's look first at the roots.

To do this, pull up one of the small plants carefully. A weed will do just as well as any other plant. You might have to loosen some of the dirt around it before you start pulling. This way, you won't damage its roots.

The roots look like a little tree upside down! There are many branches going out from each big branch. Some of the branches are so thin, you can hardly see them!

Plants need roots to do two very important jobs. One job is to hold the plant in the ground. Remember how hard you had to pull to get it out?

The other job the roots do is to feed the plants. This is how they do it.

Each root is covered with a very thin skin. Water from the soil can go right through this skin easily. Mixed with the water are minerals which the plants need if they are to grow.

If the roots did not take in the water and the minerals, the plants would die. They cannot take in water any other way except through the roots. No matter how much water you put on the leaves, the plants cannot use it. This is why *every* plant needs roots.

Some plants make their roots do a third job. They pack food into them just in case some is needed later on.

Do you have carrots or beets growing in your garden? If you do, pull one up and look at it. See the thick root of the beet or carrot? This is where the plant packed away some extra food. This food is so good, we eat it ourselves!

3

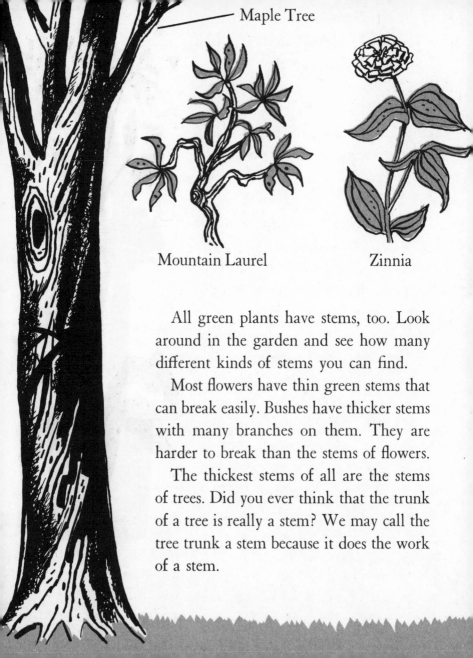

Maple Tree

Mountain Laurel   Zinnia

All green plants have stems, too. Look around in the garden and see how many different kinds of stems you can find.

Most flowers have thin green stems that can break easily. Bushes have thicker stems with many branches on them. They are harder to break than the stems of flowers.

The thickest stems of all are the stems of trees. Did you ever think that the trunk of a tree is really a stem? We may call the tree trunk a stem because it does the work of a stem.

What does the stem do?

Its first job is to hold the plant up from the ground toward the sun. A little plant does not need a strong thick stem to hold it up. But a great big plant, like a tree, needs a very, very strong stem to keep from breaking. Can you see that the bigger the plant is, the thicker and stronger its stem is?

The stem's other job is to carry water and minerals from the roots to the leaves.

You can prove this for yourself. Break the stem of a plant in the corner of your garden. Can you squeeze out some water?

There is a better way to prove that the stems carry water to the leaves. Ask your mother to give you a stalk of celery with leaves at the top. She has really given you a stem of the celery plant. Stand it in a glass of colored water. It is easy to color water by putting some food coloring in it.

5

Let the celery stand in the colored water for a day. Then you can see how the stem carried water and minerals to the leaves. They will be the same color as the water, only lighter. The stem, too, will be colored with the water it was carrying.

Some plants put away extra food in their stems. The celery is such a plant, and so is the sugar cane. People found out how good this food is and use these plants for their own food.

Now let us think about green leaves. How many different kinds of leaves can you find in the garden? Can you tell the name of a plant by looking at its leaves? Many people can. Maybe you will learn how some day, too.

6

In fact, you probably know already how to tell some plants by their leaves.

For example, when you see a tree with bunches of thin needles on it, you know it is a pine tree.

As yet, you may not be able to tell all the different kinds of pine trees there are. But when you see those bunches of thin needles on a tree, you know it belongs to the pine tree family.

You may also know marigolds in your garden by their feathery leaves as well as by their yellow flowers.

But right now, let's find out about the work of the leaves.

Green leaves are the food factory of the plant. Here, food is made out of water and a part of the air that we and other animals breathe out.

But this factory can work only in light. When it is dark, the work stops.

Here is another curious thing about the factory. The *green color* of the leaves must be present, if the factory is to make food.

Sometimes, though, you see a plant with red leaves. You may wonder, how can such a plant make food? The answer is, that even though the leaves look red, there is enough green color hidden under the red to help make food.

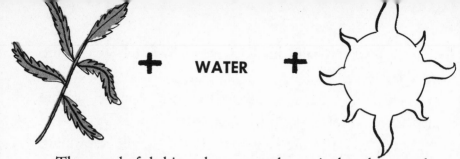

+ **WATER** **+**

The wonderful thing about green leaves is that they are the food factory for all living things. Even people cannot make their own food. They must use the food the green leaves have made, or eat animals which have eaten plants.

Green leaves know the secret of *making* food in light. They have kept the secret so well that scientists are only now beginning to find out how to make it.

When you think about it, you can see how other parts of the plant help the food factory. The roots take in the water with minerals in it. Then the stem carries this water to the leaves.

The leaves have another job to do besides making food. They do most of the breathing for the plant. On the underside of the leaf there are tiny holes that you cannot see. The plant breathes through these holes. Waste water goes out through these holes, too.

No wonder when you think of plants, you think of green leaves first! They are the most important part of the plant, and do the hardest work!

Though some plants need special things to grow, *all* plants need: LIGHT, WARMTH, WATER, and MINERALS.

Most of the plants in your garden begin to send out leaves in the spring, when it gets warm. Even those that stay green all winter look a little different in the spring and summer.

In your garden, look at a pine tree or a bush that did not lose its leaves last winter. We call such plants "evergreens." Do you see new little green pine needles or bright new green leaves growing? Though these plants stay alive all winter, they do not grow in the cold. They wait until it gets warm.

Have you ever wondered where those first weeds come from early in the spring? The seeds were already in the ground all winter long, waiting for it to get warm enough to grow.

Did you watch some plants grow last summer, and then see them seem to die? If you did, you were probably surprised to see these same plants come up again in the springtime, even though you did not plant a single seed.

What really happened last autumn was this. The top of the plant, above the ground, *did* die. But the roots stayed alive. When it got warm, the roots sent up a new stem and leaves. Violets and hollyhocks that grow in many gardens are such plants.

11

Can you think of other plants in your garden whose roots and stems, too, stayed alive? They may have *looked* dead, but in the spring you found out they were very much alive.

Of course — trees and bushes! In the summer, so much food was packed away in the stem and roots, that there was enough for the winter, too.

If you know how, you can tell that trees and bushes are alive in winter. Look at the branches carefully. See if you can find the tiny buds which will open into leaves when it gets warm.

All green plants need plenty of light, too. The leaf factory, remember, must have the light to make food. When days are long in the summer, the plants are in the light longer and can grow better.

When the days grow shorter, the leaves have less light to make food. Then the plant gets ready for winter. Some store food away in their stem and roots, or some just die.

You know, of course, that your garden needs water. If there is no rain for a few days, you water it yourself. But did you know that the plants in your garden need certain minerals too? They use these minerals to grow strong and healthy.

Good soil has plenty of these minerals in it. But as plants grow they use up the minerals in the soil. Then you must put back more of them if you want your plants to grow well.

You do this by putting "plant food" or fertilizer, into the soil. This way you help the flowers and vegetables grow better.

Flowers, Fruit and Vegetables

We grow plants because we want either beautiful flower or fruit, or vegetables. Sometimes, if the garden is big enough we can grow all three.

Let's talk about flowers first.

Besides being beautiful, do they have any job to do for the rest of the plant on which they grow? Are they useful?

Yes indeed. Almost all green plants need flowers to make seeds. If no more seeds were made, you would not be able to have new flowers next year. Even those flowers that grow from the same roots each year once started from seeds.

How does the flower make seeds?

Rub your finger on the inside of a flower in the garden. Has some yellow powder come off on your finger? If not, try another flower until you do get some.

The yellow powder is called *pollen*. It grows on tiny stalks in the middle of the flower. When the pollen gets ripe, it can rub off on to anything that touches it. It can be blown around by the wind, too.

If you are allowed to pick a flower in your garden, do so. With your thumb-nail, cut open the thick part at the bottom where the petals join the stem.

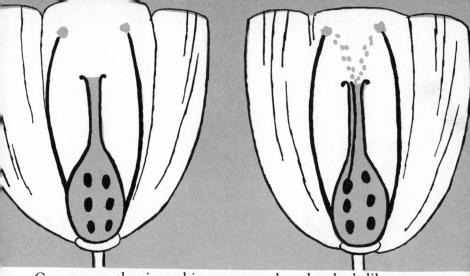

Can you see the tiny white or green dots that look like un-ripe seeds? They are really tiny eggs which may indeed become seeds after a while. Now try to find the little stalk at the top of the "box" where you found the eggs. The stalk ends inside the flower, near the pollen-stalks.

When pollen falls on the top of the stalk of the seed-box, each little pollen grain starts to grow. Each one sends a long tube down from it into the seed-box. Then, when a tube reaches a tiny egg, it fertilizes the egg. Now the egg can begin to grow into a seed.

As it grows, the plant packs some good food around each seed and gives it a strong coat. A ripe seed is really a baby plant with food packed around it, wearing a strong coat.

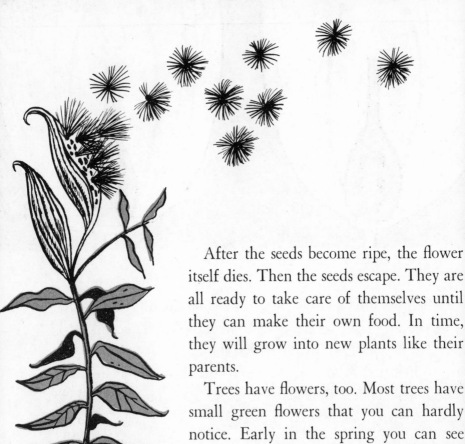

After the seeds become ripe, the flower itself dies. Then the seeds escape. They are all ready to take care of themselves until they can make their own food. In time, they will grow into new plants like their parents.

Trees have flowers, too. Most trees have small green flowers that you can hardly notice. Early in the spring you can see them on the trees before the leaves have grown big. Have you seen tree-flowers all over the ground when a strong wind blows?

You may have seen tree-seeds, too. Acorns are the seeds of oak trees. The seeds of maple trees have little wings on them that help them float through the air. You may have called these "polynoses" when you played with them.

If there is a fruit tree in your garden, you surely have seen tree-flowers. Do you remember what happens after the blossoms fall from the tree?

After a few weeks you can see tiny fruits — apples, for example — growing where the blossoms were. When the apple gets ripe, break it open. There you can find the seed, inside the fruit.

Can you guess what part of the flower has become the fruit? It is the seed-box itself, where the seeds grew.

Many vegetables, too, are really ripe seed-boxes. Think about some of the vegetables that may grow in your garden.

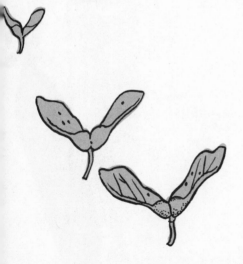

Tomatoes and cucumber plants first have flowers. Then, when the flowers die, tiny tomatoes or cucumbers begin to grow. When these become ripe, you eat them. What you are eating are the seeds together with the box in which they grew!

What part of the plant do you think string beans are? Can you see that a string bean is also a seed-box with the seeds still inside?

Sometimes you eat only the seed of a plant, and throw away the box. Are you surprised to learn that peas, beans, and nuts are seeds?

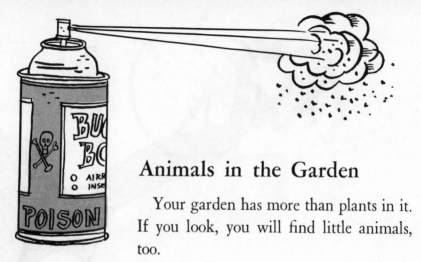

Animals in the Garden

Your garden has more than plants in it. If you look, you will find little animals, too.

It may be hard for you to think of insects, bugs, earthworms, and birds as animals. But they *are* animals, just as dogs and cats are.

Some of these little animals are harmful. The most harmful are insects. They eat parts of plants and sometimes cause them to die.

To get rid of harmful insects, a gardener has to spray his plants with insect poison. But many of these poisons are harmful to people, too. NEVER PLAY WITH INSECT SPRAYS. Until you know much more about them, say to yourself,

"Stay away from insect spray."

But there are some very useful insects, too. One of these is the lady-bug. This round little orange bug with black dots on its wings loves to eat small insects. It eats the tiny bugs that harm roses and other flowers.

Another helper in the garden is the praying mantis. Have you ever been frightened by this big, ugly insect? You need never again be, for it will not hurt you. The praying mantis eats so many harmful insects that it is the garden's good friend.

21

We must also not forget the help the garden gets from most birds. Though birds may eat cherries and berries in the garden, they also eat harmful insects.

It is a good idea to put a bird-house in the garden. In the spring, a bird may build its nest in the bird-house. Then, when the little birds hatch out of the eggs, watch the parent birds. They catch hundreds of insects and bring them to the nest to feed the baby birds. They love to bring worms from fruit trees.

Among our animal friends in the garden are the earthworms. They dig into the soil and make it loose. As they dig, they turn the soil over and bring air into it. This gives the roots air to breathe.

Also, when the soil is loose, plants can get water more easily from it. When it rains, water sinks down into loose soil better than into hard soil. The loose soil holds the water for plants to use when it is not raining.

As earthworms dig into the soil, they carry tiny bits of dead plants with them. This helps fertilize the soil and spread its minerals around.

So you see, worms have another use than simply as bait for fishing!

Have you seen a bee buzzing around flowers? It has been attracted to the flowers because of the bright colors and the sweet smell. The bee is looking for the nectar that it needs to make honey.

The bee finds nectar inside the flower at the top of the seedbox, near where the pollen grows. As it brushes against the pollen, it pushes some on to the top of the seedbox. A lot of the pollen sticks to the bee, too.

Then, when the bee goes on to another flower, it drops pollen inside the other flower. In this way, flowers have a better chance of making seeds.

Before you kill any little animal in your garden, ask yourself, "Is it useful, or is it harmful?"

In the winter when your garden is asleep, it needs to be covered with a warm blanket. Almost every winter, the garden gets just such a blanket — of snow.

Even though snow itself is cold, it covers the ground and helps keep the warmth inside so the seeds and roots don't freeze.

As the snow melts, water from it slowly sinks into the ground. The water does not run off from the ground as it does after a heavy rain.

Your garden stays warmer and wetter than it would without snow. Then, when spring comes around, you can plant seeds again.

Your garden is ready to grow again.